Introduction

Some instructors may tell you that they can teach you the "right" way to paint, but the truth is that there are many different techniques, and what's right for you is really a matter of personal discovery based on the kind of art you want to create. Since I was a child, I've been preoccupied with producing realistic drawings of human faces. As I began to explore oil painting, my search was for a technique that would allow me to create fine details while also bringing a sense of life to my skin tones.

I studied some of the techniques of other artists--both living and dead--through workshops, videos, books, and online research. I became particularly interested in the classical technique of **verdaccio**, which involves the painting of a "dead" layer that establishes the values in the skin tones before the final layers of color are applied. My own technique evolved to incorporate concepts I picked up from other artists as well as approaches I learned through my own trial and error.

In writing this book, my goal was to transform my technique into a straightforward system that could be applied with relative ease, so that others can learn from my experience just as I have learned from artists who preceded me.

Oil is not exactly simple, however, and some basic understanding of the interactions between paints and mediums is required if you are to paint effectively. Thus, I begin this book with a discussion of materials and fundamental techniques for preparing the canvas, glazing, and varnishing.

The bulk of the book, however, is composed of three demonstrations showing the production of three paintings from initial drawing through to final result. (For those who are not yet comfortable drawing directly on their canvas, the first of these demonstrations shows how to transfer a drawing from paper to canvas.) By following these demonstrations, you can see exactly how my initial draw-ing evolves and how I mix my palette at each step of the glazing process. You will also see how the same basic approach will work for a variety of different skin tones.

How you use this information ultimately is up to you. Certainly, you could try following my technique as a rigid system for creating your own artworks. I hope, instead, that you'll use it as a jumping off point for exploring and refining your own technique. Enjoy!

Materials list

OIL PAINT

I use Gamblin oils, except Burnt Sienna
I use Winsor&Newton

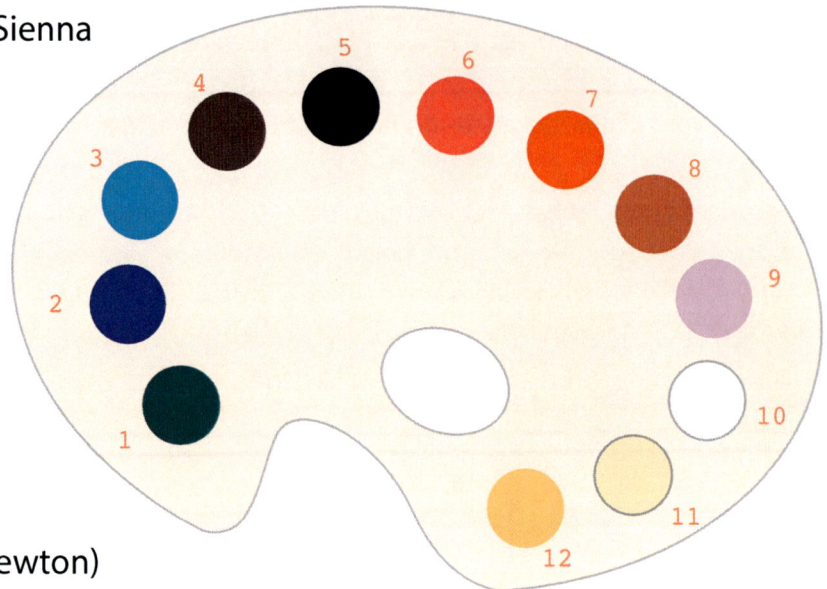

1. Sap Green
2. French Utramarine
3. Cerulean Blue
4. Burnt Umber
5. Ivory Black
6. Permanent Rose
7. Cadmium Red
8. Burnt Sienna (prefer Winsor&Newton)
9. L color (stands for Lavender)

    Is a mixture of:
      1/4 French Utramarine
      1/4 Permanent Rose
      2/4 Titanium White

10. Titanium White
11. Naples Yellow Hue
12. Yellow Ochre

(and Zinc White for glazing technique)

ACCESSORIES:
• Paper towel roll
• Palette
• Palette knives
• 3 small jars to hold medium
• Sandpaper (120 grit)

MEDIUMS
• Turpenoid (odorless)
• Refined Linseed Oil
• Gloss Varnish (Winsor & Newton)
• Liquin

BRUSHES:
• Synthetic Mongoose, Prefer
• Princeton Art & Brush Co. brand
• Round: Size 0, 2, 4, 6 (one each)
• Filber: Size 4, and 6 (one each)
• Flat: Size 2, 4, 6 (one each)
• Fan: Size 4

SURFACES
Belgian Linen (primed linen canvas)
or Primed acrylic gesso canvas

Preparing canvas

The method for preparing a canvas varies from artist to artist. This is primarily because there are several options from which to choose in every phase of preparation. Here, I just want to outline what I do to prepare for my oil painting.

I use both of the most common canvases, cotton and linen, with linen being the more expensive. Both kinds of canvas can be purchased primed or unprimed, but I like to buy them primed to save time.

Primed canvas allows you to skip the process of mixing and applying the sizing and ground. However, unprimed canvas is less expensive, and frequent painters find it beneficial to learn how to apply their own priming.

Sometimes I add a few more coats of gesso to create a smoother finish. Since I love details, the smoother the surface, the better.

Gesso dries rapidly, so it must be applied quickly in smooth, even strokes in one direction. After the first coat, allow the gesso to dry (approximately one hour) and lightly brush with fine sandpaper to smooth. After smoothing, wipe the surface with a soft, dry cloth or a soft brush to remove dust and residue. To avoid ruining your brush, you should also thoroughly rinse your brush between applications because gesso cannot be removed once it dries.

For sandpaper, about 120 grit should work well. Anything larger (80 grit) leaves gouges, while anything finer (400 to 800) will take forever. Make sure you sand all of the high spots.

Toning canvas

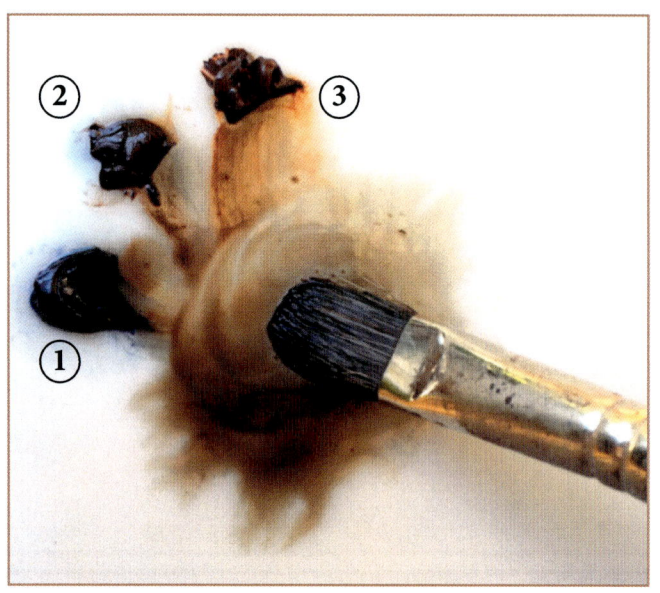

1. *French Ultramarine*
2. *Burnt Umber*
3. *Burnt Sienna*

Toned canvasses make it easier to establish correct tones for your painting. The background color on the canvas will act as your mid-tone and it becomes easier to establish the lighter lights and darker darks.

Toning is optional. I find the white of the canvas distracting, and it's more difficult for me to control the values for my painting. By toning it, the intensity of the white canvas is minimized, and this helps me to see the colors more clearly.

If you start with a white canvas, dark tones will appear darker than they are and you may struggle to establish light areas because you can't get lighter than the white of the canvas.

Step 1. Have some parts of French Ultramarine, Burnt Umber, and Burnt Sienna on your palette. For a warmer tone, add more Burnt Sienna. For a cooler tone, add more French Ultramarine Blue.

Step 2. Using a brush or paint knife, mix all three colors together. To thin the mixture, dip your brush in Turpenoid. Scrub the mixture all over your canvas or linen.

Step 3. Use paper towels to remove some of the excess oil. This process will lighten your canvas. I like to have my canvas at mid-tone value.

It's a good idea to tone your canvas at least 24 hours prior to beginning painting.

Oil paint mediums

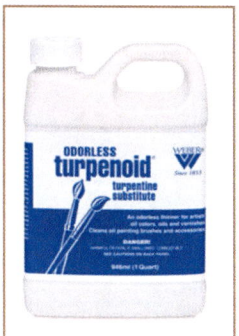

TURPENOID
Turpenoid is a odorless mineral spirit (OMS) solvent. It is used to thin paints and clean brushes. Turpenoid and Linseed Oil is usually combined to make a great medium.

LINSEED OIL
Linseed oil is the most basic and traditional medium to be mixed with paint. Adding more linseed oil will extend your paint, while also making it more liquid, which will make it more transparent. Additionally, it will slow down your dry time considerably.

REFINED LINSEED OIL
Adding Refined Linseed Oil to colors increases flow and slows drying times. It can be mixed with Tupentnoid to create a traditional slow-drying painting medium

STAND OIL
Stand oil is a thickened version of refined linseed oil. It increases flow and gloss and slows dry time. Colors mixed with stand oil will dry to a smooth, enamel-like finish.

DRYING MEDIUMS
There are a variety of products available, and it is advisable to research which ones work best for you. I like to use **Liquin** to speed up drying time for my work when needed.

LIQUIN IMPASTO
Linquin Impasto is a medium used to thicken oil paint to add more texture and body.

GLOSS OR MATTE VARNISH
Gloss varnishes are chosen because they give the brightest, deepest colors but works with gloss varnish have a lot of reflection. Matte varnishes avoid reflections but the colours appear duller. Your painting must be completely dry before you can apply varnish.

DAMAR VARNISH
Damar is the final varnish and should never be used as a medium.

Portrait in Oil with Cuong Nguyen

Fat over lean rule: avoiding cracks

If you are building up your painting in layers, you need to know about the "fat over lean" rule. It is very important that each new layer have more oil on it than the previous layer. The reason for this is that canvas naturally expands and contracts with the weather. If you have a stiffer (leaner) layer on top of a softer (fatter) layer, the fat layer will tend to expand and contract more than the lean layer on top, and the painting will crack.

For the first layers or base layers, such as my under-painting (verdaccio), I like to mix 3 parts Turpenoid with 1 part linseed oil. I mix this combination in a small jar and label it #1 for the first layer. After the first layer dries, I'm ready for the next.

For the second layer I like to mix 2 parts Turpenoid and 2 parts linseed oil. I store this in its own jar with a #2 label. Organization is key so that when you walk away from your painting you will be able to return and know what layer comes next.

For the third layer, when I get a lot more detailed, I like to use a mixture that is 1 part Turpenoid and 3 parts linseed oil. The higher oil level will help the painting have that shiny look that all oil paintings have. Place this mixture in its own jar and label it #3. This is also the mixture I use for the "oiling out" technique, which will be discussed later.

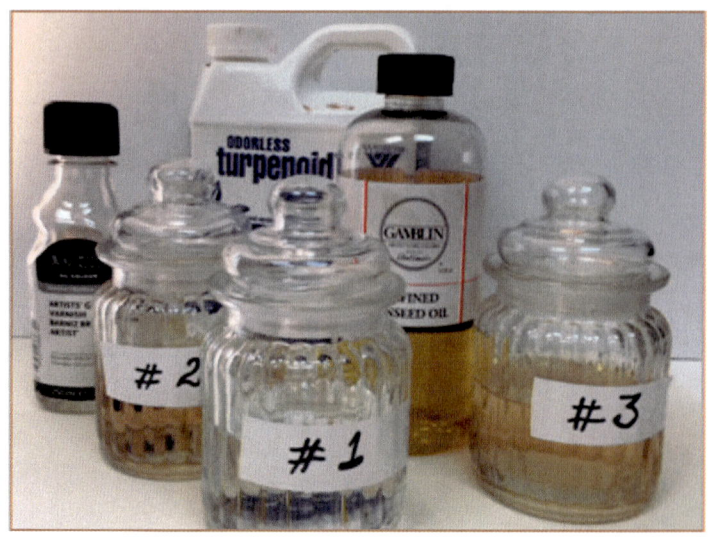

You can find many different ready-made mediums in the stores. It's OK to buy them for your convenience, but for me, the best medium is the one that you can modify to suit your own needs. It's not hard to create your recipes, and I'll give you suggestions based on what I've tried and have found works best for me. For this ebook, my focus will be on simple and efficient recipes.

Keep in mind that the more Turpenoid you use, the faster your paint will dry.

1/4 Linseed Oil + 3/4 Turpenoid

Under-Painting

2/4 Linseed Oil + 2/4 Turpenoid

For Skin tone

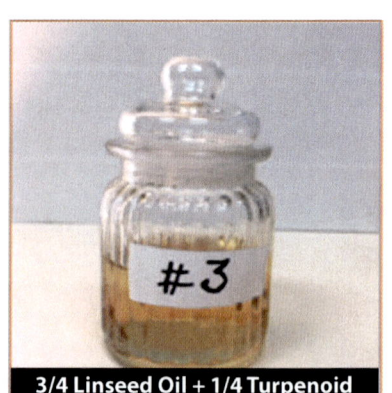

3/4 Linseed Oil + 1/4 Turpenoid

**Oiling Out
Glazing**

Verdaccio - underpainting

Verdaccio is the Italian name for the mixture of black, white, and yellow pigments resulting in a grayish or yellowish (depending on the proportion) soft greenish brown.

A true verdaccio technique generally refers to the approach used by Italian fresco painters, who would use egg-tempera paints in their plaster frescoes. An initial green-gray layer of paint would be balanced by subsequent layers of pinkish tones.

This Italian technique, however, had similarities to a technique popularized by Flemish oil painters. Flemish painters using the *"dead layer"* technique would actually start with a bone color composed of Raw Umber and Yellow Ochre, and then glaze over it with a layer that had tones from white to olive green to black. This created a sense of illumination in the final piece once the final skin colors were added.

The palette I use for my underpainting technique includes Burnt Umber, Ivory black, Yellow Ochre, and Titanium White. You will find more information in the demos in this ebook.

(Detail of painting by Ugolino di Nero in Certaldo's sacred art museum, photo Lisabelle)

1. Burnt Umber
2. Ivory Black
3. Yellow Ochre
4. Titanium White

Oiling out technique

Oiling out technique help to brighten dull areas and prevent "sinking"

1. Refined Linseed Oil
2. Odorless Turpenoid
3. Make-up sponge

When you complete an oil painting, you may notice that certain areas appear more glossy while others appear flatter than others. This usually occurs due to what is known as "sinking," when the top layer of oil has been lost to the layer underneath. There are 3 common causes:

1. An over-absorbent surface
2. Using too much solvent
3. Not enough medium

Using the "oiling out" technique can give the painting a new lease on life. Unfortunately, as you build up oil color in layers, the different drying rates can also result in a paint film with varying degrees of absorbency. This shows up as dull spots rather than a complete dull area. The trick is to treat these dull areas as soon as they are dry. I use my mixed **medium #3** (3/4 Linseed Oil + 1/4 Turpenoid), sparingly applied to make-up sponge or a clean cloth, which is gently rubbed into any sunken areas. Wipe off any residue and leave it to dry for a day or two.

You don't have to wait until your painting is complete to "oil out." Rather, you can do it in between as well. **Please do remember that your painting must be completely dry before you can apply this technique.**

Oiling out should be done before you varnish your painting!

Glazing technique

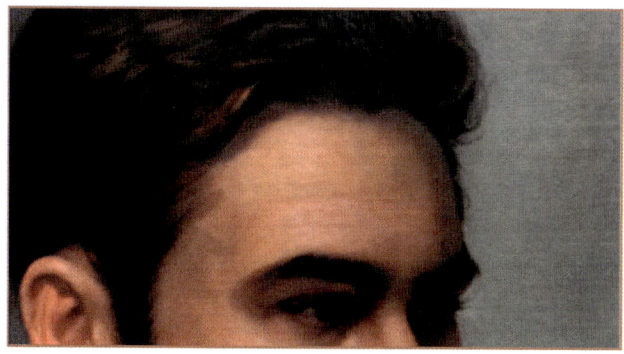

Before glazing

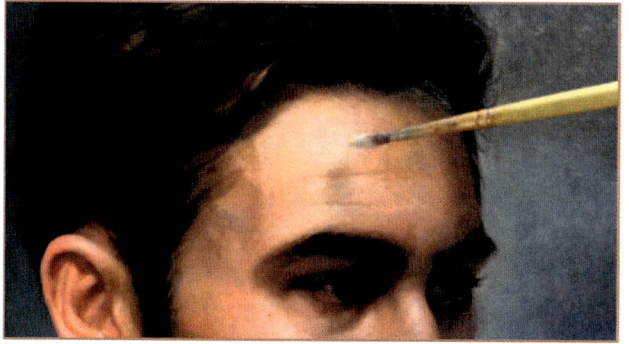

After glazing

Glazing creates a unique "shine through," stained-glass effect that is not obtainable by direct mixture of paint. It's the perfect technique for painting the complexities of skin tones.

Glazing is a technique that has been employed by painters since the invention of oil painting. Leonardo Da Vinci and Vermeer are well-known for this technique.

A glaze is thin transparent or semi-transparent layer of oil applied with a soft-bristled brush over another thoroughly dried layer of opaque paint. Glazes can modify the appearance of the underlying paint layer. Glazes also change the value, hue and texture of a surface. The beautiful thing about glazing with oil paints is that that the appearance of the colors when glazed one on top of the other, is different than when the colors are mixed together.

Glazes consist of a great amount of binding medium in relation to a very small amount of pigment. Drying time will depend on the amount and type of paint medium used in the glaze. Different mediums can increase or decrease the rate at which oil paints dry.

Most oil paints are opaque, and painters will add special medium or a lot of medium to the paint to make it more transparent for the purposes of glazing.

You can find many different ready-made mediums for glazing in the stores. It's OK if you want to buy them for your convenience. For glazing, I prefer to create a simple recipe: 3/4 linseed oil + 1/4 Turpenoid, and I call it **medium #3**. You will learn more more about my techniques throughout the demos.

Varnishing

To ensure your finished oil painting continues to look its best, adding the right varnish in the right way will be a sound investment. Varnish protects the painting from dirt and dust and evens out the painting's final appearance, making it all equally glossy or matte.

Over the years dirt and dust will stick to the varnish rather than the painting and when necessary, the varnish itself can be removed and the painting re-varnished to look as good as new.

Often gloss varnishes are chosen because they give the brightest, deepest colors, but works with gloss varnish have a lot of reflection. Matte varnishes minimize reflections, but the colors appear duller. Be sure to complete the following steps before you begin varnishing:

1. Artist's Gloss Varnish
2. 1"1/2 Medium Brush

1. Wait until your painting is completely dry.
2. Choose a dust free area in which to work, keeping windows and doors closed.
3. Keep the work to be varnished flat on a table or work surface – avoid working vertically.
4. Use a flat, wide, soft, tightly-packed varnishing brush. Keep it clean and use it only for varnishing.
5. Stir the varnish well and pour it into a clean flat saucer or tin and load your brush. Wipe it on the side of the saucer so it is not dripping.
6. Apply the varnish in 1 to 3 thin coats rather than one thick coat.
7. Use long even strokes from top to bottom while moving from one side to the other, and remove any bubbles.
8. Once you leave an area, avoid going back over areas that you have done. For those areas that you have missed, simply allow them to dry completely and re-varnish.

Wait until your painting is completely dry!

Demonstrations

Demo 1: "Chelee and The White Rose"
oil on linen 14"x16"

DRAWING STUDY

The most traditional way to start a painting is do a drawing study. By spending time doing a drawing, you will learn more about the characteristics of the model, as well as learning the color values. It also helps you to create a better composition when you transfer the drawing to canvas.

I spent about 6 hrs to make this drawing study of Chelée,. I used only HB and 3B graphite pencils on white drawing paper.

TRANSFER THE DRAWING TO TRACING PAPER

The next step is transferring the drawing study to tracing paper. First, I placed the tracing paper on top of my drawing of Chelée and used artist archival tape to attach the top two corners to secure the paper.

To trace the outlines of my drawing, I used a charcoal pencil, 3B medium, and carefully traced the outlines. The pressure I suggest is light to medium, because pressing too hard might damage the original drawing.

I continued to draw the main outlines of my drawing study of Chelée - no need to focus on details at this point.

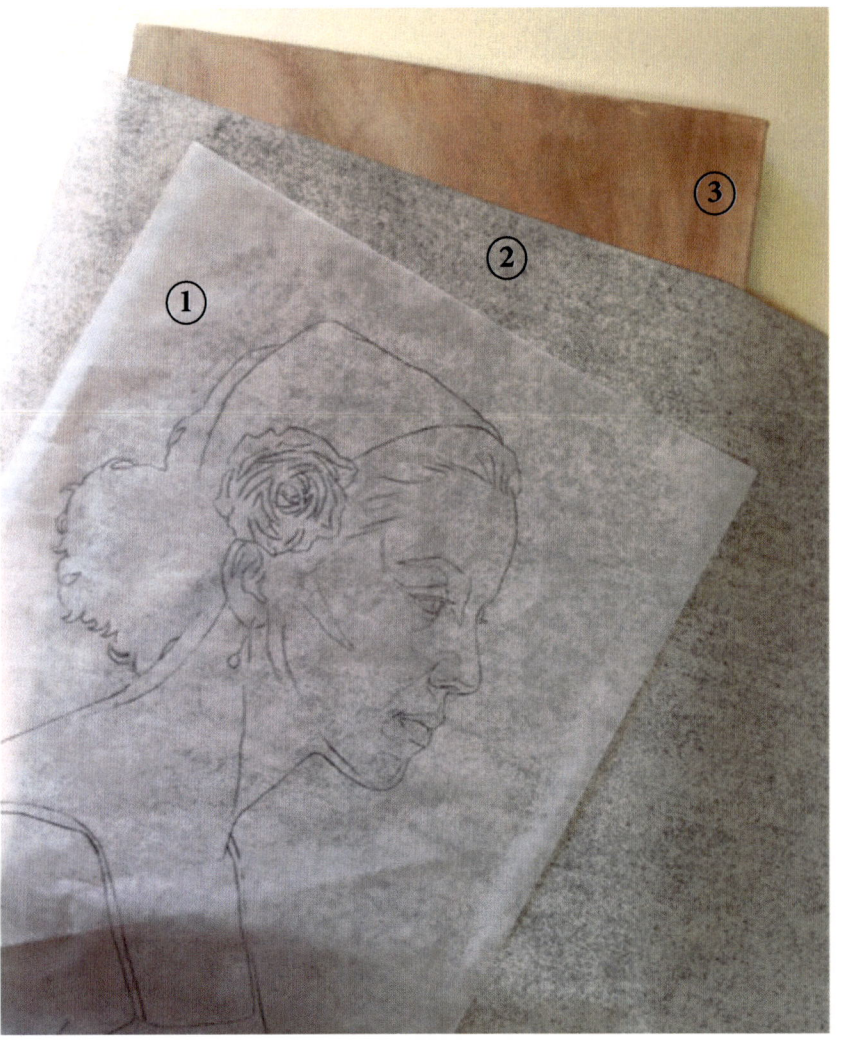

1. Outline image
2. Carbon paper
3. Tonned canvas

TRANSFER THE OUTLINES TO CANVAS

I like to sand and tone my canvas the night before so it's ready to be used. To transfer the outlines to the canvas, I make sure that I have my drawing placed in the desired composition on the canvas, then insert the carbon paper in between them. To avoid movement of the papers, I use artist archival tape to affix the corners.

After securing the papers by taping the top corners, I used a ballpoint pen to trace the outlines onto the canvas. I used medium pressure, and flipped the paper up from time to time to make sure the outlines were going through the carbon paper to the canvas.

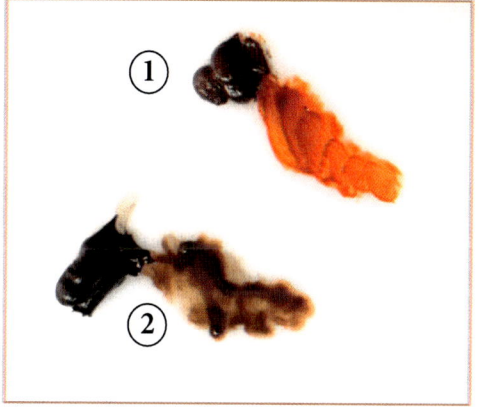

1. Burnt Sienna
2. Burnt Umber

RE-DRAWING WITH PAINTS

After the outlines had been transferred to the canvas, I started to re-draw them with paints. Initially, I used Burnt Sienna, but later used Burnt Umber to darken the shadowed areas.

I continued to re-draw the outlines with Burnt Umber and Burnt Sienna. I wanted this stage to dry quickly, so I used Turpenoid to thin out the paint at this point. Upon completion of any drawing, I let it dry before I can start the next step: Verdaccio.

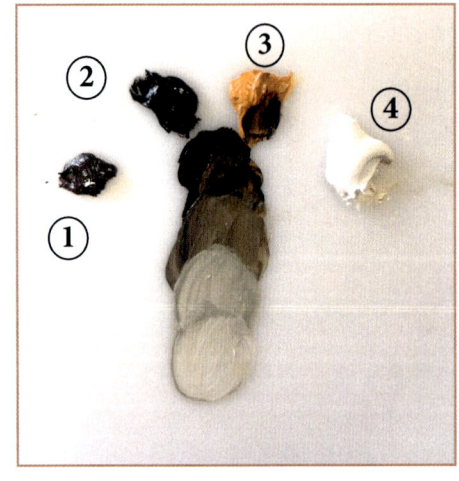

1. Burnt Umber
2. Ivory Black
3. Yellow Ochre
4. Titanium White

UNDERPAINTING - VERDACCIO

To start my underpainting, I used the combination of Burnt Umber, Ivory Black, Yellow Ochre, and Titanium White. I mixed the colors with **medium #1** to 5 values, from dark to light.

At this stage, I was focused 100% on values, as I paid close attention to Chelée's anatomical structure. I also filled in the background at this time.

After finishing this underpainting stage, I would have to wait for the painting to completely dry before I could start the next steps. Generally, it takes from 1-2 days to dry. Sometime I add some Liquin to the paints to speed up this process (it will dry overnight).

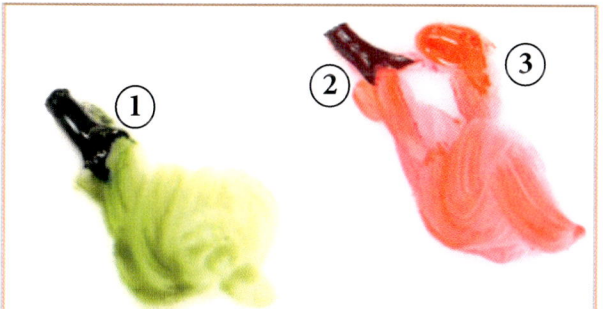

1. Sap Green
2. Permanent Rose
3. Cadmium Red

ADDING TEMPERATURE

After the painting had completely dried, I started adding the temperature on Chelée's face. First, I used a combination of Permanent Rose and Cadmium Red for her nose, her cheek bones and around the eyes. Second, I added a thin layer of Sap Green on all of the shadowed areas. I used **medium #2** for this stage.

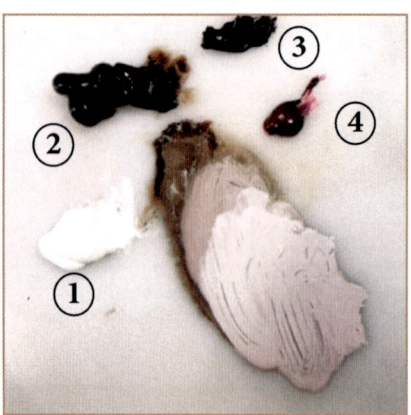

1. Titanium White
2. Burnt Umber
3. Ivory Black
4. Permanent Rose

ADDING COLOR TO BACKGROUND

Before beginning to work on the skin tone, I added some colors to the background. I wanted the background to relate somewhat to the white rose which Chelée is wearing, so I used a combination of Titanium White, Burnt Umber, Ivory Black, and Permanent Rose. I used **medium #2** to mix the colors to 3 different values, from dark to light. I started to apply the light value around her face, and gradually applied the darker values toward the top and the bottom of the canvas.

1. Sap Green
2. Permanent Rose
3. Burnt Sienna
4. L color

GLAZING THE FIRST SKIN TONE COLOR

After applying the color to the background, I started glazing the first skin tone color on Chelee's figure. I used **medium #3** to mix Sap Green, Permanent Rose, Burnt Sienna, and L color (notice that L color is the only opaque color). **Medium #3** *(3/4 linseed oil + 1/4 turpenoid)* helped to make the mixed color transparent. I used a round brush #2 to apply this combination on Chelée's entire figure.

The picture on the left shows how the skin tone looked after I had added the first skin tone color. For this technique, patience is the key. I needed to set the painting aside to dry before I could apply the next layer.

APPLY THE SECOND SKIN TONE COLOR

After the painting had dried, I applied the second layer of skin tone, using a combination of Burnt Sienna and L color for the middle tone. For the shadowed areas, I applied a thin layer of the combination of Burnt Umber and Sap Green. I also started rendering her facial features.

Portrait in Oil with Cuong Nguyen

1. Titanium White
2. Burnt Umber
3. Ivory Black
4. Permanent Rose

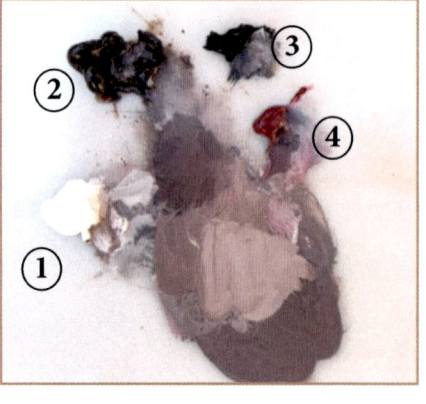

At this stage, I decided to work on her scarf. Using the same color palette which I had used for the background, I added a little more of Permanent Rose and White. I started from dark to light to control the values.

For the rose, I continued to use the same color palette. Working from dark to light, big shapes to small shapes, I saved the details for last.

I also worked on Chelée's hair at this stage. I wanted to avoid using straight black. Instead, I mixed Sap Green, French Ultramarine, and Burnt Umber to create a deep, dark color.

Working from dark to light, I applied this mixed color first, followed by Burnt Umber. I highlighted her hair with a combination of Burnt Sienna and Yellow Ochre.

Once I had finished her hair, I added some details on her scarf, using my brush #0.

1. *Cerulean Blue*
2. *Sap Green*
3. *Burnt Umber*

I continued to work on Chelée's neck and shoulder. I used the color resulting from the mixture of the colors listed above.

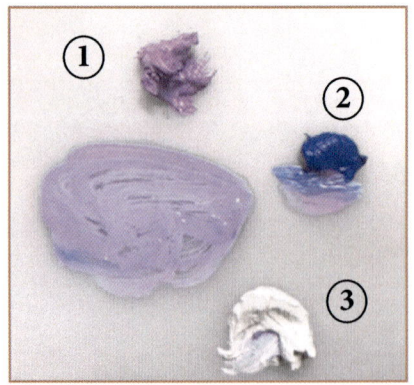

1. L color
2. Cerulean Blue
3. Zinc White

For the highlight on Chelée's shoulder, I used a combination of Cerulean Blue, L color, and white.

Again, it was time to wait for the painting to **dry completely** before I could use the *"oiling out"* and *"glazing"* techniques.

OILING OUT

To continue to work on Chelée's portrait, I used the "oiling out" technique to brighten dull areas, simply applying a small amount of **medium #3** on the entire painting with a make-up sponge.

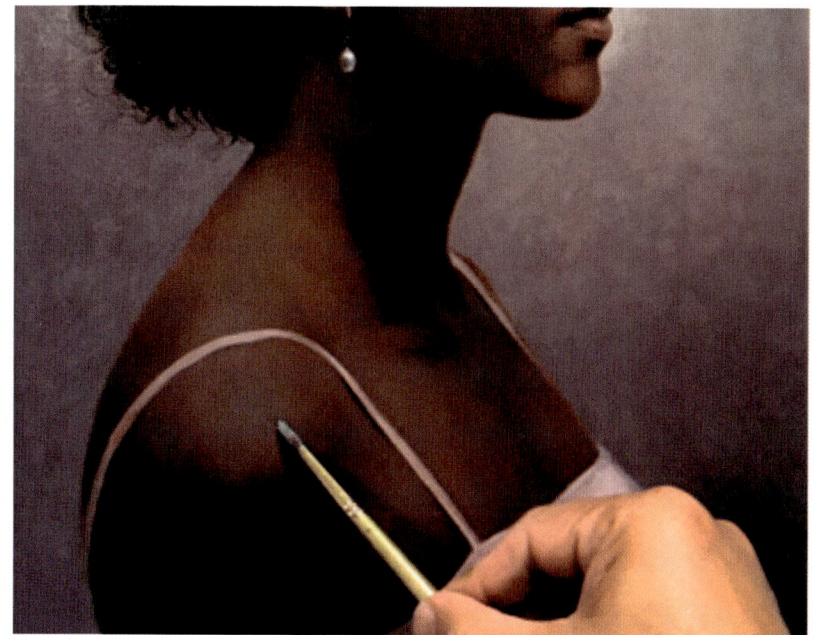

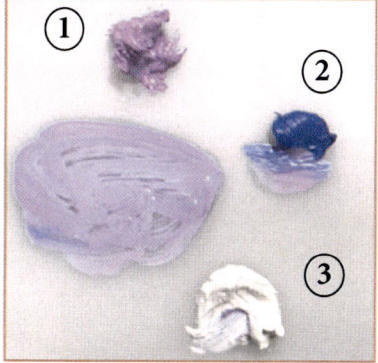

1. L color
2. Cerulean Blue
3. Zinc White

GLAZING

When it was time for me to apply the glazing technique on the highlights of Chelée's forehead and shoulder, I used Zinc White to mix with L color, and Cerulean Blue. Zinc White is the least opaque white, making it ideal for tints and glazing. It also has the stiffest consistency.

I used **medium #3** to make the color more transparent. Dipping an old brush #6 into the mixed color, I wiped most of the color off of the brush onto a paper towel. I applied the color lightly to the desired areas until I was happy with the results. Then, I allowed the painting to dry. Four weeks later, I varnished it with gloss varnish from Winsor & Newton.

"Chelée and The White Rose - Oil on linen - 16"x14"

Demo 2: "Portrait of |Michael"
oil on linen, 11"x14"

Portrait in Oil with Cuong Nguyen

1. Burnt Sienna
2. Burnt Umber

DRAWING

For this demo, I skipped the drawing study stage, and I used my brush (flat #6), starting with Burnt Sienna to sketch the image. I thinned out the paint by mixing it with Tupernoid. When I was happy with the proportions, I continued to draw with Burnt Umber to darken the drawing and give it more details. At this stage, I was focusing on color values. It's essential to get your drawing correct, so you need to take your time sketching your model. It's important to go back to measure frequently to ensure you've got the right proportions at all times.

Portrait in Oil with Cuong Nguyen

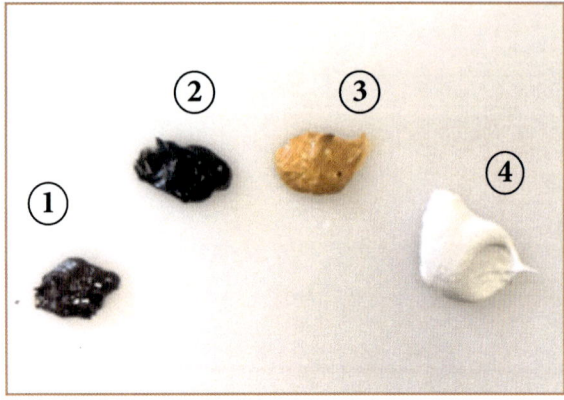

1. Burnt Umber
2. Ivory Black
3. Yellow Ochre
4. Titanium White

UNDERPAINTING (VERDACCIO)

To begin my underpainting, I used the combination of Burnt Umber, Ivory Black, Yellow Ochre, and Titanium White, mixing the colors with **medium #1** to 5 values, from dark to light.

At this stage, I was focusing 100% on values, while also paying close attention to Michael's bone structure and muscles.

Once I had finished this underpainting stage, I would have to wait for the painting to **completely dry** before I could start the next steps. Usually, it will take from 1-2 days to dry. Sometime I add some Liquin to the paints to speed up this progress (it will dry overnight).

1. Sap Green
2. Permanent Rose
3. Cadmium Red

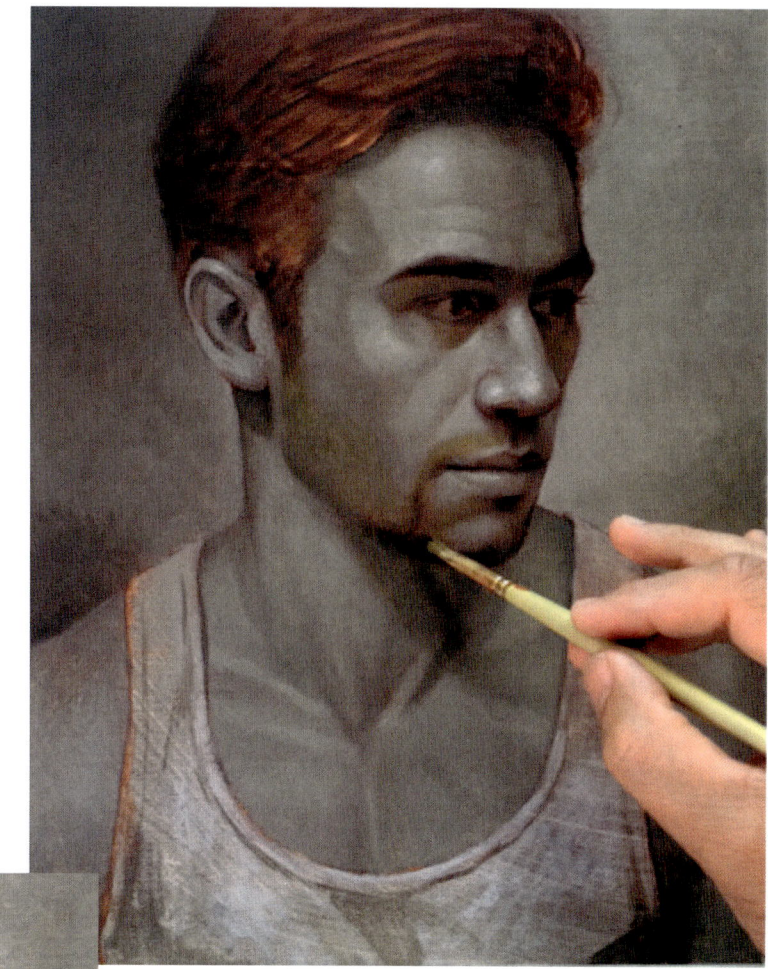

ADDING TEMPERATURES

After the underpainting had completely dried, I started adding cool and warm colors on Michael's face. It is important to notice that a person's skin tone is never one color. There are always parts a bit warmer, and parts a bit cooler. If you paint the entire face with the same color, the portrait will look like a doll face.

For Michael's face, I started by adding a thin, translucent layer of Sap Green (by mixing with **medium #2**) in the shadowed areas. Next, I added a thin layer of Permanent Rose mixed with Cadmium Red around his eyes, nose, lips, ears and cheek bones.

I allowed the colors to settle for about 30 mins before starting to apply the first layer of skin tone.

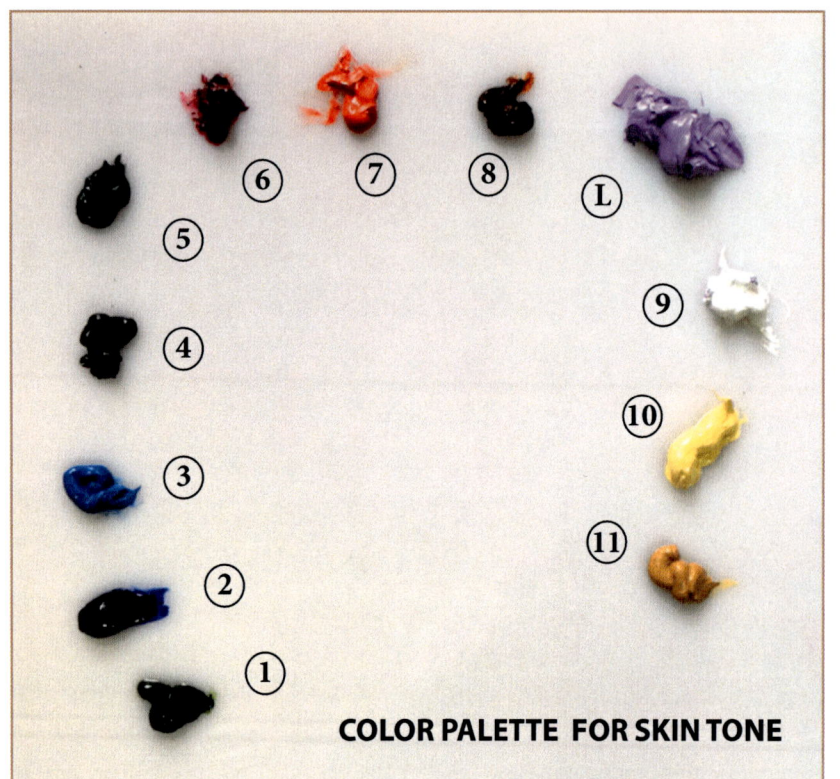

COLOR PALETTE FOR SKIN TONE

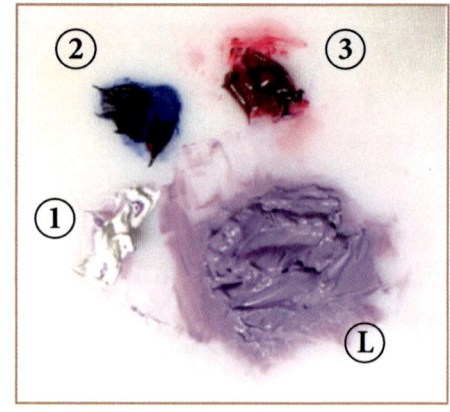

1. 2/4 of Titanium White
2. 1/4 of French Utramarine
3. 1/4 of Permanent Rose

1. Sap Green (transparent)
2. French Utramarine (transparent)
3. Cerulean Blue
4. Burnt Umber
5. Ivory Black
6. Permanent Rose (transparent)
7. Cadmium Red
8. Burnt Sienna (Semi transparent)
L. Mixed Lavender
9. Titanium White
10. Naples Yellow Hue
11. Yellow Ochre

ADDING FLESH COLORS

First, I started with (L) color, adding Burnt Sienna, and finally Naples Yellow. Mixing them together with **medium #2**, I had a combination color for the first layer of skin tone. I used brush #2 for this stage.

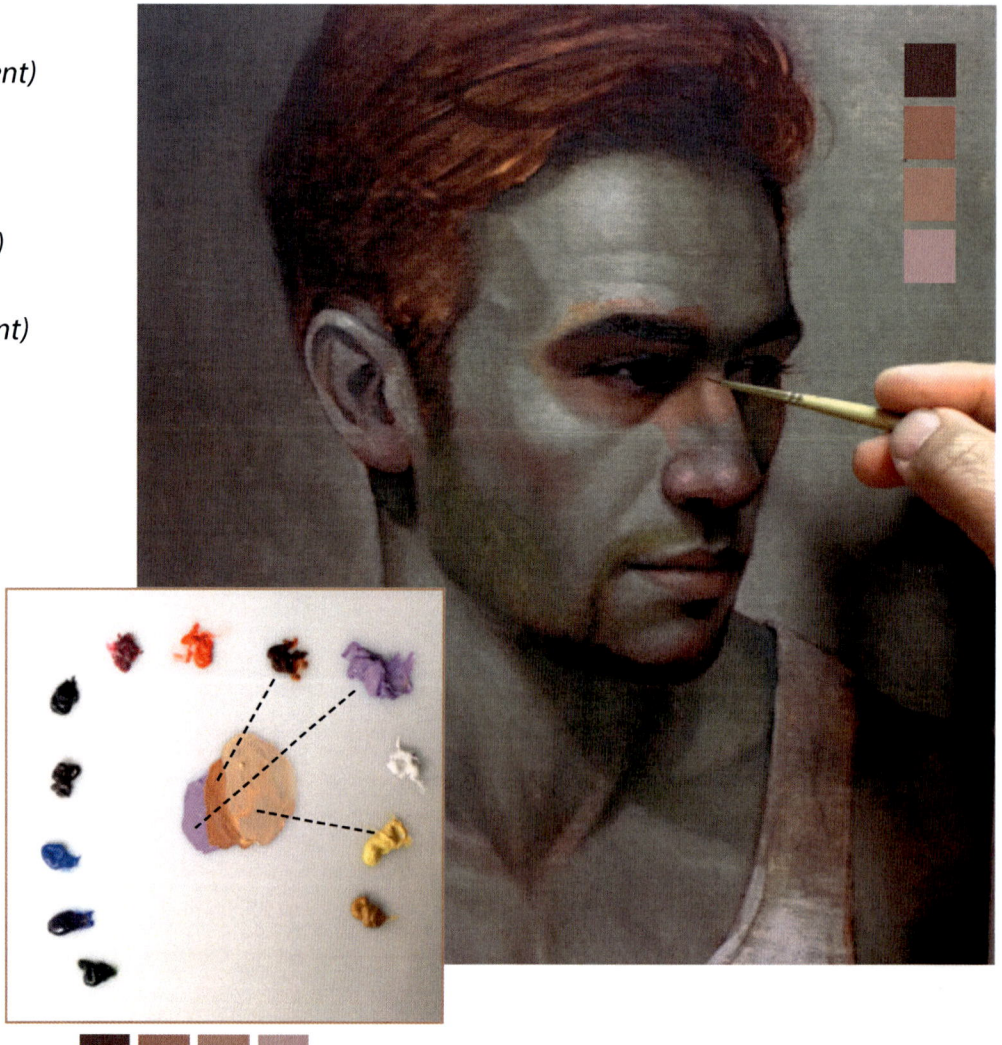

I continued filling in Michael's face with the skin tone color. For the shadowed areas, I added a combination of Burnt Sienna and Sap Green. For the highlighted areas, I used the combination of L color mixed with Naples Yellow and White. Adding **medium #2** helped to make the color transparent.

To separate Michael's face from the background, I added a thin layer of a combination of Black, French Ultramarine, and White. Later, I will add more paint to the background. I used a flat brush #4 for the background.

Portrait in Oil with Cuong Nguyen

Sap Green

I added more Sap Green on Michael's beard and shadowed areas before applying the skin tone color. For his hair, I used a combination of Burnt Umber, French Ultramarine Blue, and Sap Green to create a deep black. For highlighting, I used Burnt Sienna and some Yellow Ochre.

OILING OUT TECHNIQUE:
The next day the color had sunk, becoming flat and dull. To continue working on Michael's face, I used the "oiling out" technique to brighten dull areas, simply applying a small amount of **medium #3** to the color areas with a make-up sponge. Remember, the first layer of color has to be **completely dry** before you can use the "oiling out" technique.

Sap Green

After "oiling out," the colors returned. I added a thin layer of Sap Green on the shadowed area under his chin. I continued building up the color in the shadows by using the combination of Burnt Umber, Burnt Sienna, Cerulean Blue and Sap Green.

To control the value for the painting, I added the second layer for the background, using the combination of Burnt Umber, French Ultramarine, Ivory Black, and White.

1. Sap Green
2. Burnt Umber
3. Burnt Sienna

For the details on Michael's beard, I used a small brush (#0). I avoided the use of black, instead mixing Sap Green, Burnt Umber, and Burnt Sienna. This resulted in a very nice dark color. I also used this combination for the shadows of his hair.

1. Ivory Black
2. French Utramarine
3. Titanium White

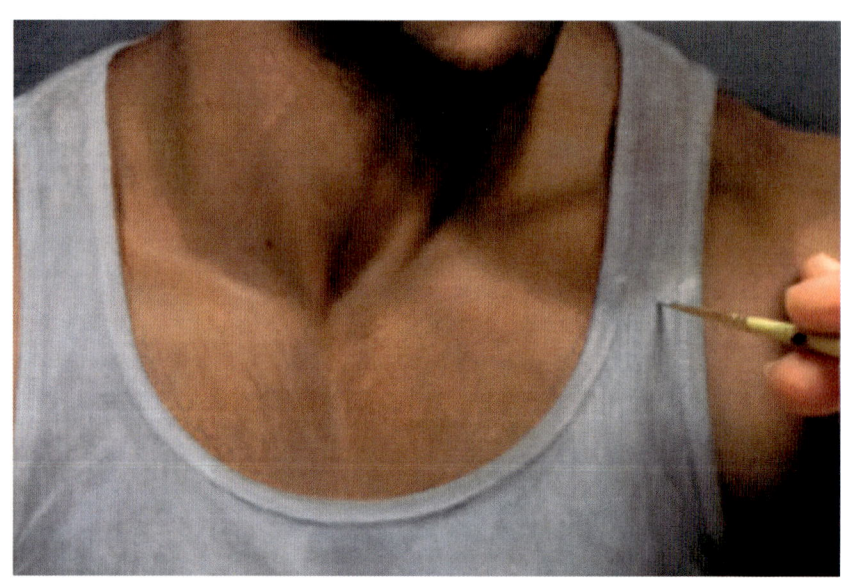

Next, I decided to work on Michael's tank top. Even though his tank-top is white, I tend to avoid using straight white. Instead, I used cool light grey by mixing Black, French Ultramarine, and Titanium White. The reason not to use straight white is to avoid flatting out the values. I only use 100% white for the highlighting of white fabrics.

At this point, I set the painting aside for 2 days so it could be **completely dry** for the next step: *glazing!*

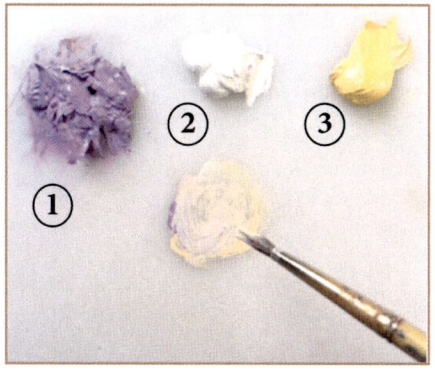

1. Mixed Lavender
2. Naples Yellow Hue
3. Zinc White

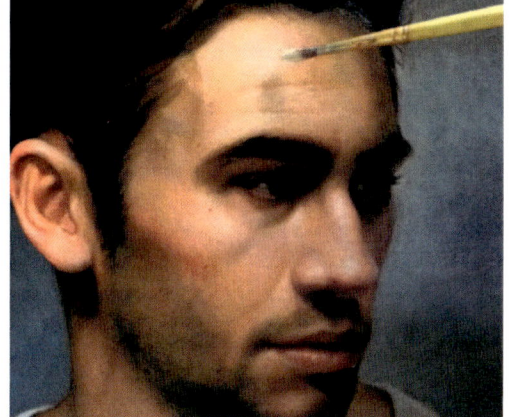

GLAZING

Michael's painting was now dry and I could start the glazing process. I used Zinc White mixed with L color, and Naples Yellow. To make the resultant color more transparent, I added **medium #3** to the mixture.

Using an old brush (#6), I dipped it into the mixed color, wiping most of the color off the brush onto a paper towel. I lightly applied the color to the desired areas until I was happy with the results. In this case, the areas highlighted were Michael's forehead, his cheekbones, his nose, and his shoulders.

Again, I allowed the painting to dry. Four weeks later, I varnished it with a gloss varnish from Winsor & Newton.

Michael, Oil on linen, 11"x14"

Portrait in Oil with Cuong Nguyen

Demo 3: "Kristina"
oil on linen, 11"x14"

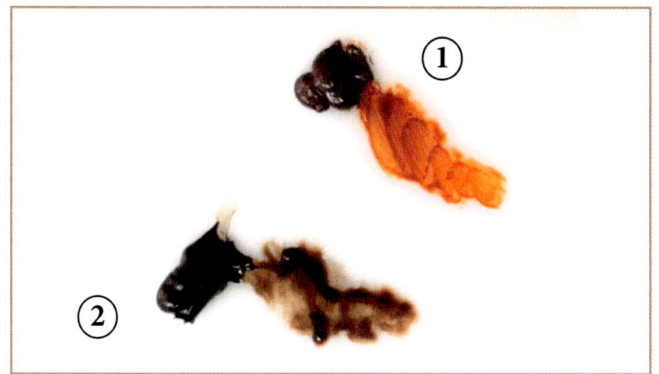

1. Burnt Sienna
2. Burnt Umber

DRAWING

To prepare my canvas for this demo, I sanded and toned it the prior night. Starting with my flat brush # 4, I sketched straight to the canvas using Burnt Sienna.

This is a very important stage, so at first I focused on the tilt of her head. Next I worked on forms, shapes, and values. Details came last.

(If you're not comfortable using a brush to sketch, you can use charcoal, charcoal pencil or pastel pencil for this stage.)

1. Burnt Umber
2. Ivy Black
3. Yellow Ochre
4. Titanium White

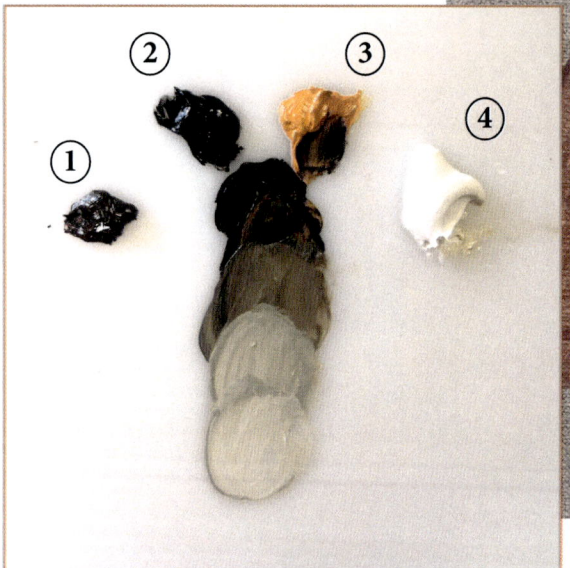

UNDERPAINTING - VERDACCIO

I waited until my sketch was dry so I could start the underpainting. I mixed Burnt Umber, Ivory Black, Yellow Ochre, and Titanium White to 5 values, from dark to light. For this stage, I used **medium #1**.

Once I had finished this underpainting stage, I set the painting aside to dry before I could start the next steps. Depending upon the temperature in your studio and the brands of colors you use, it might take from 1-2 days for your piece to dry. Sometimes I will add some Liquin to the paints to speed up this process (it will dry over night).

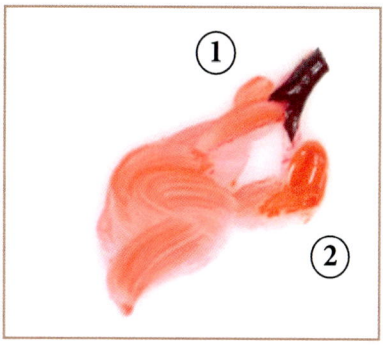

1. Permanent Rose
2. Cadmium Red

ADDING TEMPERATURE

Remember that a human's skin tone is not all one color. The flesh color changes depending on lighting, temperature, and emotions. Some parts of the face are warmer while others are cooler. In general, the area around the eyes, the nose, cheekbones, and lips are warmer than the rest of the face.

For this stage, I used a combination of Permanent Rose and Cadmium Red. I added **medium #2** to thin out the paints. I used a round brush #2, lightly applying the mixture on Kristin's eyes, nose, lips and cheekbones.

Sap Green

I continued to apply a thin layer of Sap Green to the darker areas, particularly the shadows on the left side of her face, her neck, and some of her shoulder.

FIRST LAYER OF SKIN TONE

For this stage, I used the color that results from the mixture of L color, Burnt Sienna, and Naples Yellow. I used **medium #2** for this stage.

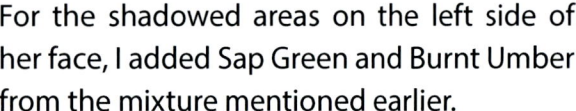

For the shadowed areas on the left side of her face, I added Sap Green and Burnt Umber from the mixture mentioned earlier.

Portrait in Oil with Cuong Nguyen

Sap Green

The shadow of the jaw on Kristina's neck is strong. Before applying the skin tone color, I added another layer of Sap Green.

Then it was time for me to add the skin tone color on Kristina's neck and shoulders. I used **medium #2** to mix Sap Green, Burnt Sienna and L color for the shadowed area. For the mid-tone areas, I added some Naples Yellow.

1. *French Ultramarine*
2. *Cerulean Blue*
3. *Black*
4. *Titanium White*

ADDING BACKGROUND

Next, it was time for me to add colors to the background.

First, I mixed a combination of French Ultramarine, Cerulean Blue, Black, and White to create 3 different values of cool grays. Using brush #4, I started working from dark to light.

I set the painting aside for 2 days so it could **dry completely** so I could start the next processes: "oiling out" and "glazing".

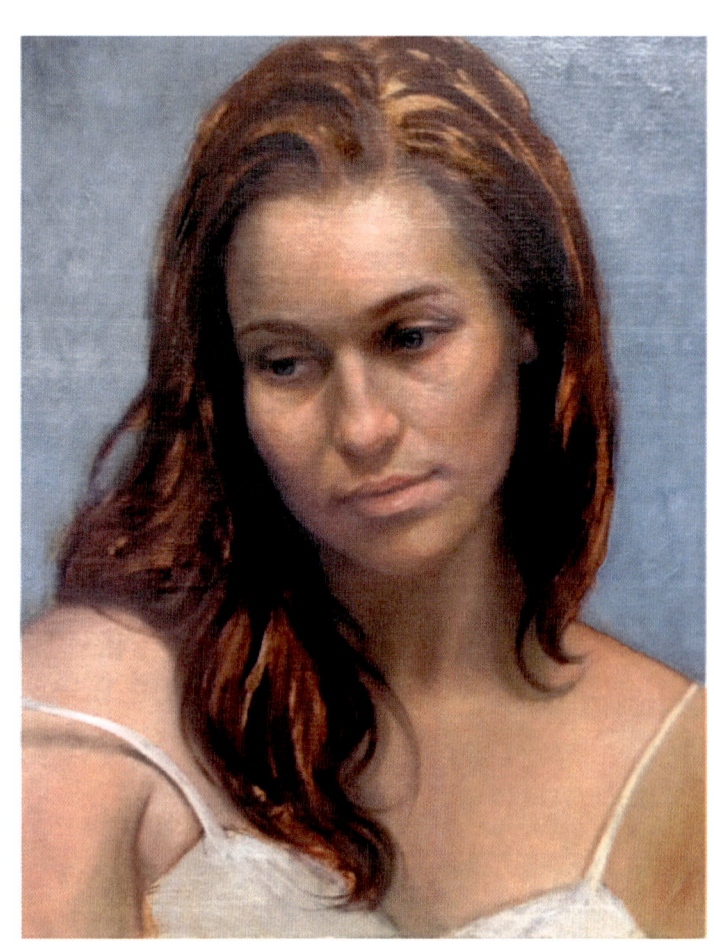

Portrait in Oil with Cuong Nguyen

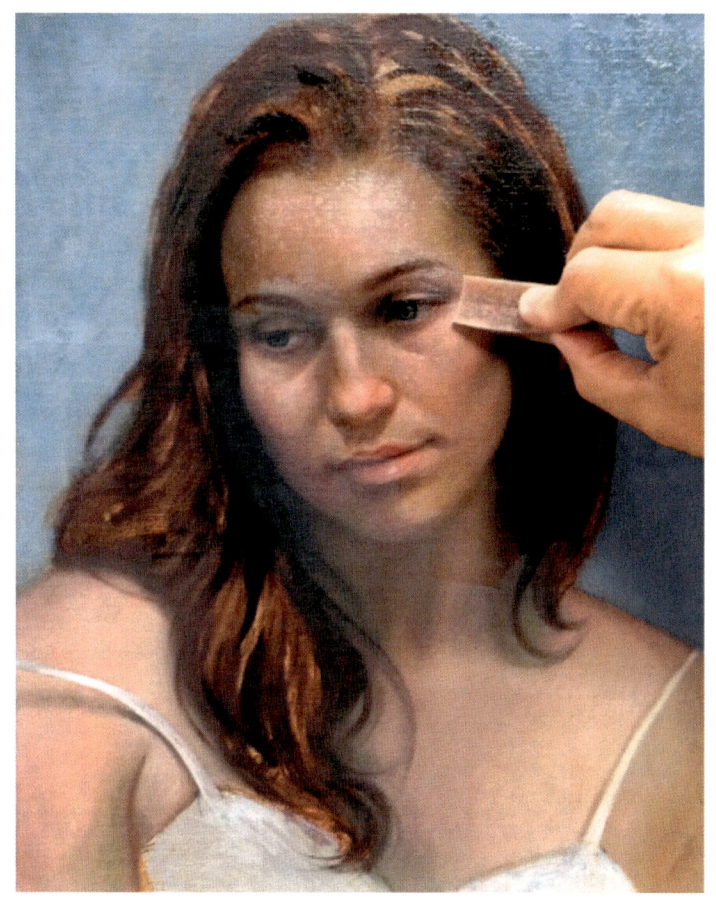

OILING OUT TECHNIQUE:
After a few days, the color had sunk, becoming flat and dull. I used the "oiling out" technique to brighten dull areas by applying a small amount of **medium #3** on the color area with a make-up sponge.

GLAZING

I used Zinc White mixed with L color, Burnt Sienna and Naples Yellow. To make the resultant color more transparent, I added **medium #3** to the mixture. I dipped an old brush #2 into the mixture, wiping most of the color off of the brush onto a paper towel. I lightly applied the color to the desired areas until I was happy with the results. In this case, the areas highlighted were Kristin's forehead, her cheekbones, her nose, and the muscles above her lips.

Sap Green

ADDING COLORS TO HER HAIR

Don't be afraid of adding colors to the hair. In this case, I added Sap Green in the shadowed areas of Kristina's hair. I also added a combination of Permanent Rose, Cadmium Red, and Burnt Sienna.

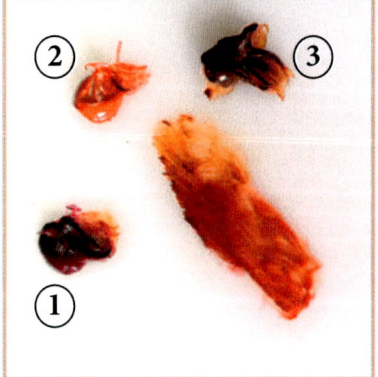

1. Permanent Rose
2. Cadmium Red
3. Burnt Sienna

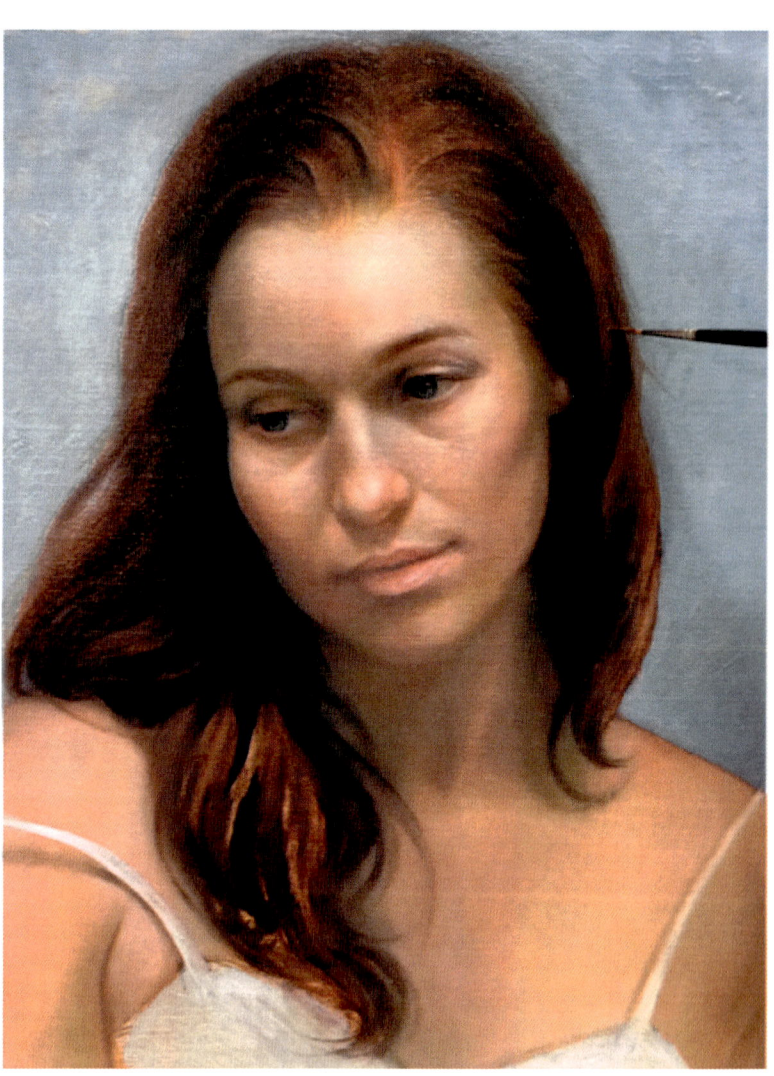

For the highlights in her hair, I used a combination of Burnt Sienna and Yellow Ochre.

GLAZING HER SHOULDER

Next, it was time for me to apply the glazing technique to her shoulders. I used the combination of L color, Burnt Sienna, Yellow Ochre, and White.

ADDING FLECKLES

The last thing I added was some freckles on Kristina's skin tone. As a redheaded woman, her skin has lots of freckles. Personally, I think her freckles add character and beauty to her features.

I mostly used Burnt Sienna mixed with Sap Green for her freckles, and I used my tiny brush #0 for this process.

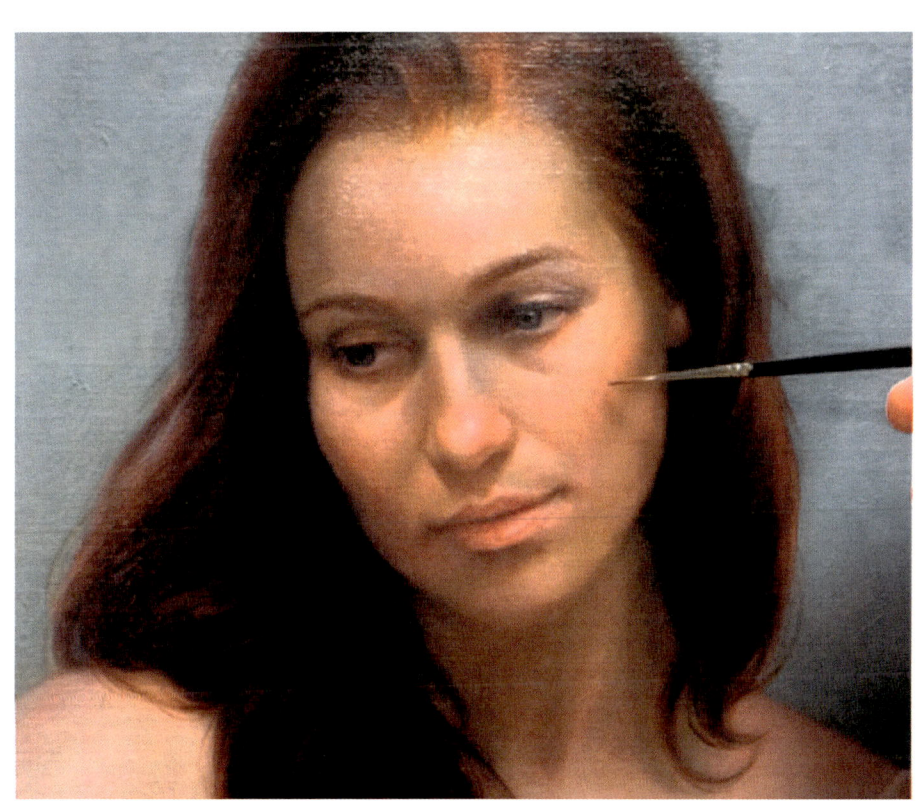

VARNISHING

After 4 weeks, the portrait of Kristina was completely dry and ready to be varnished.

I choose gloss varnishes because they give the brightest, deepest colors. After 24 hrs, the painting was ready to frame!

"Kristina"
Oil on linen
11"x14"

Some of cuong's work...

"Preoccupied"
Oil on canvas
24x30"

"Siri"
Oil on linen
16x24"

"Sean in Profile"
Oil on linen
16x26"

"Paul as Leonardo"
Oil on linen
16"x24"

"The Artist's Model"
Oil on linen
24"x36"

About Cuong Nguyen

Cuong Nguyen's ability to highlight the beauty in the world around him is something that informs his art as well as his perspective. One might say that he represents the opposite of the tortured artist cliché: despite the fact that his formative years in Vietnam were characterized by significant hardship, his sometimes romantic and sometimes mysterious portraits and still life paintings reflect his positive outlook and determination to persevere.

Growing up in poverty after the fall of Saigon, Cuong's greatest pleasure was finding time to draw. At a young age, he earned extra money for his family by doing street portraits, and he was accepted to Saigon's Academy of Art while in high school. Even as a child, Cuong was fascinated by the human face, and his single-minded practice of drawing eyes and other features rewards us today with portraits that have a spark of life to them.

His study at the Academy of Art in Saigon was interrupted when he had the opportunity to emigrate to the U.S. in 1991, and the challenge of establishing himself within a new country and culture temporarily distracted him from his love of fine art. He earned a degree in illustration from San Jose State University and established a successful career as an icon designer with a prominent Silicon Valley Web company.

Ultimately, though, his passion for fine art resurfaced. It began first as a new hobby—participating as an artist at public street painting festivals, creating ephemeral artworks as large as 16' x 24'. Cuong soon established a reputation for painting amazingly lifelike portaits on asphalt, and he was invited to participate in festivals around the world. More importantly, though, this activity brought him back to painting, and he was soon back in his studio endlessly refining his technique with more traditional media.

Cuong earned status as a Master Pastellist with Pastel Society of America, Distinguished Pastellist with the Pastel Society of the West Coast, and Masters Circle with IAPS. He has had one-man shows at the Triton Museum and the Los Gatos Museum, both in California, and his work has been featured in both national and international competitions exhibiting worldwide.

Cuong shares his techniques through workshops taught at his own studio in California as well as those hosted by art institutes and ateliers elsewhere in the U.S. and throughout the world. For more information on Cuong's teaching schedule, visit his website at icuong.com.

Acknowledgments

I'd like to thank:

Models
Chelée Spence
Michael Robert Lazzarini
Kristina Marie Mc

Editing
Elizabeth Connor
themarginatrix.com

Translation
Oscar Lopez

My tutorial video for
pastel is available at:
www.icuong.com

facebook: icuong
instagram: icuong
youtube: cuongnguyenart
www.icuong.com

Made in the USA
Middletown, DE
27 May 2025

76144697R00031